MY FIRST LEARNING SERIES
WEATHER

Written and Illustrated by Caroline and John Astrop

U.S. Edition copyright ©1995 Modern Publishing, a division of Unisystems, Inc.
® Honey Bear Books is a trademark owned by Honey Bear Productions, Inc.,
and is registered in the U.S. Patent and Trademark Office.
All rights reserved.
No part of this book may be reproduced
without written permission from the publisher. All rights reserved.

Text and illustrations ©1993 by Caroline and John Astrop.
Originally published by Regency House Limited.

Modern Publishing
A Division of Unisystems, Inc./New York, New York 10022
Printed in the U.S.A.

It is a hot sunny day.
Tim is making a big splash in the pool.
What do you do on a sunny day?

Which creatures like sunshine?

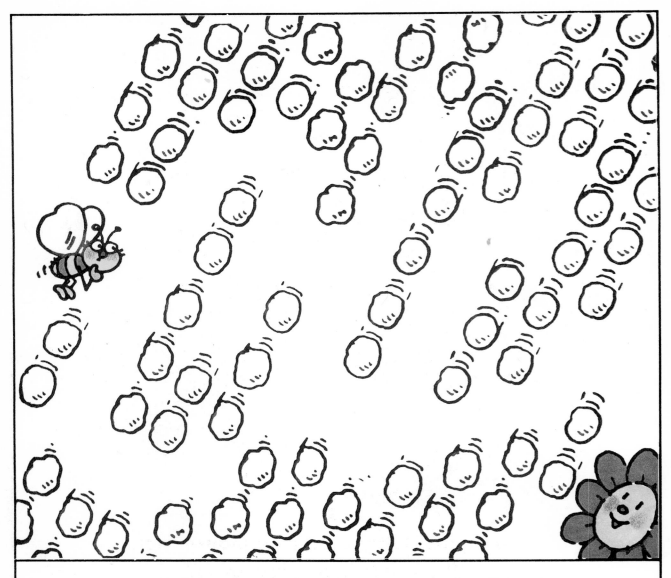

Help Bertie Bee find his way to the flower.

Hailstones clatter on the doghouse roof.
Who is inside the doghouse?
What is in the bowl?

It is pouring down rain.
Are the twins wet or dry?
What color are their raincoats?

Which things don't like rain?

What is different in these two pictures?

It is the baby rabbits' first storm.
They can hear thunder and see lightning flash.
Have you seen a storm?

The pond freezes in winter.
Jane is skating on the frozen pond.
Who has fallen down on the slippery ice?
Can you see the icicles on the tree?

Which jacket belongs to each skater?

The sun and rain have made a beautiful rainbow.
Sue can count seven different colors.
Do you know their names?

Rover wants to paint a rainbow.
What color tube of paint is missing?

Tom is lost in the fog.
Puppy dog knows the way home.
Is Tom going the right way?

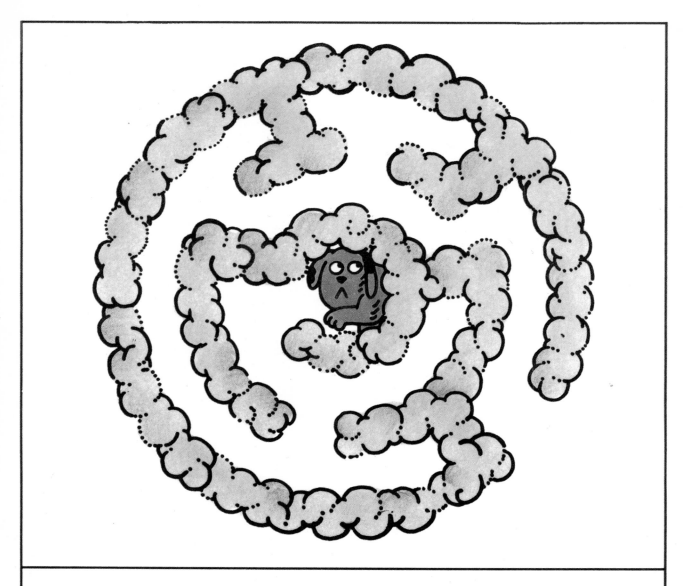

Help puppy find his way out of the fog.

Which of these things need wind?

The wind is very strong today.
What things are blowing away?
Have you tried to walk against the wind?

Everything is covered in snow.
The children are having fun.
What are they doing?

Match the pairs of snowflakes.

**These things appear in spring.
Can you say what they are?**

All of these are summer things.
What are they called?

**We see these things in autumn.
What are their names?**

These are winter things.
Do you know what they are called?

We hope you
enjoyed learning
about

WEATHER